pilgrimage

Keith Polette

pilgrimage

copyright © 2020 Keith Polette
ISBN 978-1-947271-69-2

Red Moon Press
PO Box 2461
Winchester VA
22604-1661 USA
www.redmoonpress.com

Cover photograph: Keith Polette.

first printing

For Agnes

If what a tree or a bush does is lost on you,
You are surely lost. Stand still. The forest knows
Where you are. You must let it find you.
> — David Wagoner, "Lost"

pilgrimage

From the Edge

Something calls to me from the edge of the desert, a fence of sagging guitar strings that no longer carries a tune, the scattered skulls of cows lowing to the wind, an arroyo mouthing a dry poem, stones rising out of the sand to sing of constellations that have never been named, a rusted truck turned-sphinx waiting for a lone traveler to question, a blue-tailed lizard, startled by the passing shadow of a hawk, that scurries onto the top of a rock, surveys the empty sky, and then rests like a monument to itself for the whole of an afternoon.

> hands in prayer
> a butterfly brings its wings
> together

The Game

Dusk. The children on the edge of the woods chase fireflies. A light blinks on and then off, and the children dash to where the light was, only to find the darkness has re-sealed itself. And then another blink of light followed by another mad dash, only to discover the light is gone. And this game for hours: the children chasing lights, finding darkness — while I am in the house trying my hand at paint-by-numbers, but every time I try to put paint on canvas, the numbers start moving.

> homeward bound
> all the stoplights in town
> go green

The Choice

Something there is that does not love a wall.
— Robert Frost, "Mending Wall"

About fifteen years ago, a wild cotton tree took root in the small plot of land just behind the rock wall in my yard. The tree has now grown to a height of over fifty feet, and its roots have begun pushing against the wall, causing a severe curvature. If nothing is done, the wall will topple; it's only a matter of time. So, the choice: take out the tree or lose the wall.

>sound of chopping
>my daughter asks
>if trees have feeling

The Tiger

The tiger William Blake imagined, was born of sun, fashioned and forged by a fearless blacksmith who found beauty burning in ferocity. Maybe Blake was trying to name the parts of his own soul, or maybe he was wrestling with a divinity who had the rawness of heart to conjure and create such a clawed creature, or maybe he was attempting, in his questions, to come to grips with the tiger of time that eventually and savagely consumes us all. These are some of the thoughts on my mind as my daughter and I stand before the tiger pit at the zoo. Today, the tigers are inactive, not pacing as I have seen before, but instead lying in the shade like lumpy throw rugs. We watch for a few minutes, the summer sun baking our backs. My daughter tugs at my sleeve and tells me she wants to see the penguins. I take her hand, leave the tiger pit, and head towards a watery world of black and white. With each step I take, though, I sense a faint growl burning my throat.

>   gall stones
>   the coal furnace
>   full of clinkers

FISH

When I was eight, I found "The Five Chinese Brothers" in a book of folktales on my grandmother's bookshelf, and what fascinated me more than the ways in which the four older, identical brothers were impervious to the devices of death designed for them, was how the youngest of them was able to inhale the sea, hold it in his mouth — frog-puffed — and then collect the fish that were left behind. And here I paused to imagine them, the legions of fish, flopping in the mud of an endless field, their water world suddenly siphoned off, wriggling like brightly colored dancers having lost their limbs, their unblinking eyes grim with surprise, their gaping mouths screaming in silence, as the boy basketed them, while the circling gulls began their slow descent.

pawnshop
wedding rings glitter
in the window

Winter Walk

Walking in winter, beyond the trees which stand like veins against the dull sky, my breath comes out like a ghost, and my shoes crunch the ground. I fling a large stone into the stream, where it lands with splash, the kind a great bass makes in summer at dusk, as its leaps out of the water to swallow the rising moon.

> water music
> the boy beating the river
> with a stick

In Transit

My uncle, Joe Bone, says he was born on a train half way between Chicago and St. Louis. I only met him once, but he told me that because he was born in motion, every room he entered always felt like it was in transit; even standing still gave him the sensation that his legs were made of river water, the currents pulling him downstream towards a destiny that would most likely be a waterfall. Maybe that is why, one night after he had been married for only six months, he went out for cigarettes and did not return for thirty years.

>night train
>flat cars hauling
>moonlight

Under My Skin

Something under my skin is moving, not illness or disease, and certainly not something from a sci-fi film. No, it feels as though I have suddenly become an old farm house, one abandoned by its owners years ago, because the fields were too rocky to take crops, one whose shingles are flaking off, one where mice are constantly skittering behind the plaster walls. I tell the doctor about this strange sensation, and he says I have a nervous disorder. I leave his office unconvinced and don't bother to fill the prescription he wrote, because it becomes blindingly obvious to me on my way home that I don't need to swallow pills to be free of the mice moving in me. I need to swallow a cat.

> dawn
> the cat comes home
> smelling of darkness

Flight

Leaving the grocery store, I notice a brown grackle perched on the handle of a shopping cart in the parking lot. Its angular head, like a bishop on a chess board, was tilted, pointing to a movement in the sky.

A helicopter slowly whirled out of the hanging clouds, its blades thumping the air like someone beating the dust out of a rug. The grackle and I were both silent as we watched it bank away and descend low over a cluster of houses, its nose down like a dog sniffing for the trail of something it had picked up and lost. Then, it disappeared from view.

The grackle followed, lifting off, leaving the empty nest of the cart, its shape changing into a pair of hands rising into the air, while I, heavy with bags, trudged to the car, feeling more earthbound than ever, careful though, to keep an eye on the sky, while making sure I left behind nothing to track.

> darkening sky
> a shadow takes me
> by the hand

Fishing

Even though I think my father may have unconsciously wished it, he and I could never have been the subject of a Norman Rockwell painting — one where we are as content as warm socks just taken from the dryer — sitting in a wooden rowboat, blue paint flaking off its ribs, each of us holding a fishing rod, the burnished light of day upon us, as we wait for something to tug our lines, knowing that if I am the first to haul in a bass or bluegill, he will put down his rod and turn to me, his face wide and open as a catcher's mitt, help me take the fish, its scales shimmering with sun, from the hook, clap me on the back, and say, "Great catch, son!" after which, he will then turn his face momentarily to the sky like a major league outfielder who has just leaped up to catch a long fly ball, keeping a homerun from sailing over the wall.

icy roads
a tow truck pulls a car
from a ditch

KINTSUGI[1]

It seems, these days, my body is made of clay: as common as a department store cup, as crude as an ashtray formed by a child. Each morning, the spider cracks and fault lines of my mind, the missing fragments of my heart, become more pronounced. It's then I recall the times I've slid off the shelf, been deliberately dropped, or have unwittingly hurled myself to the ground. I would like to take the damaged pottery of myself to a Kintsugi master, who would use his special mix of resin and gold dust to painstakingly repair all of me that is broken. And after his work is done, and after I have paid what I owe, I would stand in the sun, my scars gleaming, resplendent and beautiful.

> lightning strike
> a new crack
> in the turtle's shell

---

1. *Kintsugi* is the Japanese art of repairing broken pottery using resin mixed with gold dust.

Pilgrimage

It took all day to hitchhike across Idaho to Hemingway's last house which sits on a sagebrush shelf overlooking the Big Wood River. It is a square house made of concrete molded to look like wood; in each wall is a large window, so the house always looks outward. I had to view the house from afar, since this was the time before the public was welcomed in. Through my telephoto lens, taking photos from the edge of the forest, I felt like I had found big prey. That night I pitched my tent in a local park. Inside I prepared to read some of Papa's tales. But before I could open the book, thunder clouds, which had been building all afternoon, broke open like a shotgun blast. In the dark, I closed my eyes and listened to the sound of stories rain down on me all night.

> after the flood
> the watermarks
> on her letter

Questions

Five hours it took us to trek the hard-packed switchbacks in the Tetons to reach Death Canyon, where we camped for three days. That was the first time I discovered I had mountain-goat legs and felt like a satyr with a backpack. Around the small fire the first night, we watched as the herringbone pattern of firs on the mountains that rimmed us fade into darkness shot-through with starlight. In the silence, sipping tea, my mind turned to a poem by Yeats, and I began to wonder where I was, why I was, and even if I would be.

> lingering questions
> a wolf pack answers
> the moon

Alaskan Nights

During winter, near the top of the world, the light is like an old man climbing the stairs. He runs out of breath a quarter of the way up and must sit down and light a candle. He drinks lukewarm coffee that he has brought from the table, as the cat curls at his feet.

> dark side of the moon
> the unexplored places
> where we live

Autumn

Autumn has finished the woods; the trees stand exposed like casino card players who've lost everything. And I can't help but think that the trees were betting on this, knowing that winter was coming, heavy with snow, to remind them how to shiver, even coated in white. And while most of them will carry the cold in their spindly branches, a few others will lie down like lovers returning to bed after having gotten up to get a glass of water.

> fallen leaves
> the curled shavings of
> a carpenter's plane

A Penny

Walking to my car in the grocery parking lot, I noticed a shiny dot on the asphalt. Coming closer, I discovered it was a new penny, its copper color beaming with sun, causing it to resemble the burning eye of a tiny cyclops. I bent down and reached for it but stopped when I saw that it was facing heads-down, a bringer of back luck if picked up. Instead, I turned the penny over, so that the beaming face of Lincoln could reflect the sky and become an invitation of better luck for the next passerby.

> autumn
> copper-colored leaves
> in the wishing well

The Pianist

The luster in her eyes has grown dim much like a pond gone gray with the last light of day. Yet, her hands retain the shape of the music they played, kicking back and forth, almost in a sprint, across the piano keys in Scott Joplin's "Maple Leaf Rag," then slowing, moving backwards, as if her fingers were learning to walk again, in Schumann's "Scenes from Childhood," until finally they disappear altogether, their skin fading into the pure light of Debussy's "Clair de Lune." And when she had finished playing, and after the long applause, all that was left of her was her black dress draped over the piano stool, the lace at the end of the sleeves barely touching the hardwood floor.

> at dusk
> I put the last of my cash
> into the homeless woman's cup

Silence

At the end of the long train pulling away, silence darkens the station, spreading across fields pressed hard by winter, to the raven roosting alone in an abandoned attic. The only sounds that have escaped the stretch of silence are the drip of a faucet in the diner that closed at ten, the cranking of a can opener in the hands of an old woman surrounded by mewing cats, and a porch swing that creaks only once, because the wind, being paper thin, cannot even conjure a whisper.

> gray morning
> the woodpecker wakes
> the day

GALILEO

Tonight, standing before the frosted window, I notice the moon, slender as an eyelash, fading in a slow descent. And I think about Galileo, not in his prime, when he witnessed the heavens whirling and darting like luminescent barn swallows cavorting in the center stage of his telescope, but later, after he had been placed in lifelong house arrest. I picture him, stumbling in his blindness, lurching from chair to table, holding the rounded head of a spoon and feeling not curved metal, but the contour of a new planet, one that sounds like a single musical note.

> whitewashed chapel
> the sun streaming through
> stained glass

"Wheatfield with Crows"

The stormy sky in Van Gogh's "Wheatfield with Crows" is described by some as "menacing"; others suggest it is an image that foreshadows the painter's death, while others, still, say it represents the existential "sadness" and "extreme loneliness" at the fin de siècle. I am no art critic, so I cannot discount what learnéd others have surmised about Van Gogh's great painting, but it has always seemed to me that the roughly textured sky, with its dark and heavy brushstrokes, which are all converging towards a misshapen lighter swirl just off center on the horizon, are not, at second glance, suggestive of churning clouds but instead of rough feathers roiling towards form. Van Gogh's sky, then, seems to me to be a ragged and violently unformed bird, one that is exploding towards being, and the mascara-heavy crows over the anguished wheat are flying feverishly towards it so that they may midwife it into becoming a great and terrible bird, one whose wings will cut the air like scythes and whose heart will beat with the will of savage divinity.

> foreclosure
> feeding the scarecrow
> to the fire

Poet Laureate

Standing on the corner in a posture borrowed from a streetlamp, with his dog lying nearby, he is the poet laureate of the homeless holding a handmade sign, black letters on bent cardboard:

> invisible man
> needing spare change
> to change

Mark the Twain

His body was the river, his pen pushing words like paddle-wheel steamers past the logjams of his time.

And the other one, S.C., the orchestrator, diffident in white suit, dressed as if summer were his only expectation.

The persistent question: which one of them rafted south with Jim, for whom he'd have gone hell, only to become, for a moment, a western Buddha adrift in currents of silver light where fish broke the surface just to catch a glimpse of his passing?

>   quiet night
>   a single oar-stroke
>   slices the moon

The Forecast

The forecasted storm never arrived, too weak to churn this far north, breaking up, instead, somewhere south of Cuidad Chihuahua. At least a sliver of Mexico received rain, the arroyos there flashing with floods for an hour or so, but here, in this desert, we wait in what has become a daily vigil, under the baking sun, for another promise of rain. Tonight, the weather woman reports that a storm is, in fact, moving our way, but then adds that we should not get our hopes up, because it has stalled at the border.

>desert heat
>field mice finding shade
>in a cow's skull

Late Night Sounds West of El Paso

A freight train drags the darkness, with the whoosh of a heavy curtain closing, past a distant dim-lit house where ranchera music, like an array of bright bats, skitters out of a small radio on a kitchen table, as a knife chopping chiles keeps a steady syncopation on the cutting board. In a vast orchard, pecans begin to drop from husks, hitting the ground like the muffled beats of a snare drum. Deeper in the desert, coyotes, with heads raised, with throats as open as pipe organs, call to the moon like supplicants begging for grace on a night that is slowly receding into silence.

>   broken doorbell
>   the woodpecker knocking
>   on my wall

After Sleep

I've hiked before dawn into the mountains for the first time in months, feeling like a bear after a long hibernation, my feet unsteady on this narrow path. My breath comes in out in chuffs, louder than I'd like, and it startles a handful of deer, causing them to skirt by me like shadow dancers entering a distant stage. The sun begins to crest the mountain, it's blazing edge like something in a Blake painting. I stop and bend down to tie my shoe. The wind, which has begun to stir, tosses a brown leaf next to my foot. I start to brush it away, but instead study it for a moment and chuckle when I notice that both of us are curling at the edges.

>   crescent moon
>   bending wood to make
>   a wheel

The Well

Here are your waters and your watering place.
—Robert Frost, "Directive"

Even though it has long been empty, I repair the broken stonework around the well, its top rim jagged like the teeth of a boxer past his prime. After having cleared away the tree limbs that have fallen there, clogging the opening, and having mixed the mortar well, I fill the cavities in the well-wall with stones, and then with mortar-bag and trowel, I fill and pack each joint until no gaps remain. After that, I stack stones on the rim and snug them down with mortar, tapping the top of each with the wood handle of the trowel. When I am finished, I stand back and look, knowing that the well will never hold rain again, but hope, that when the new stones are set and strong, I may be able to bend over the rim and speak directly to the earth untouched by light, my words falling like water where they will gather and be held in a deep and secret place. And when need be, I may go from time to time to the well I repaired and quietly draw from the reservoir of my dark self.

> heavy snow
> the silence in the rice jar
> filling the house

The Rising

Pale dawn, a pallor of light spreads across the fields. I have risen early because of a commotion on the wooden porch. It is an owl screeching, lurching in halting steps, dragging a wounded wing. When it stands still, it looks like a ship listing at sea. I put on coat and gloves and step outside. The owl turns its yellow eyes, twin suns, and meets mine. I move swiftly, toss a heavy white towel over the owl, gather it up, careful to do no more damage to its limp wing. In my arms the owl resembles an infant struggling in swaddling or a Halloween ghost too tired and hurt to head home. I place the owl in a box and tape it shut. I put the package in the front of the truck and head to the vet, an hour away. In its small enclosure of night, the owl flaps its good wing and screeches from time to time, wondering, I imagine, why there are no stars.

raven's cry
when no one knew
iron or oil

Fog

I hiked into the hills thick with fog, my breath in slow bursts merging with the sky that had lowered itself around me. On I walked, waist-deep in a sea of grey light, pushing through a thicket of silence. After an hour — or half a day — I passed a lone tree, leafless and still, which stood like the end of a sudden gesture, and here I paused to take measure of where I was and how far I had come. I could not tell how tall the tree was, since its top was obscured from view. I leaned against it, a still point in a world that seemed to have stopped spinning and breathed in the sound of the thousand-year-old call of a red deer deep in the fog. And when it stopped, as abruptly as a door closing, I found myself standing, for a moment, alone and lost inside the oldest part of myself that I have ever known.

scissor-tailed birds
cutting my longings
in half

THE HOLLOW

I found it deep in a forest hollow, a place scooped out as if by hand. The heavy stones of its body, which had once been stacked carefully into place, now sagged like the mouth of a homeless man too long on the road. The weight of time, the history of heat, and the shroud of disuse had done their work to pull the kiln, which had long ago blazed with an alchemical brightness, down to the face of the earth, where older than grandfathers, it has become a vertical garden with trees growing out of its gaps and with a heart burning nothing but green.

>   volcanic ash
>   a flower through
>   a cow's skull eye

BLACKBERRIES

Dark clots on spiked branches, these blackberries glisten with a sweetness that their thornless cousins lack. Their barbed spines are both a warning and a dare, letting you know that you will bleed with every pluck. Your fingers are pricked with each pick, droplets of blood mixing in with the honeyed clumps gathered in the bucket, the mound of them looking like a disassembled

brain, and since this is not your first blackberry summer, you know to keep the level low, lest the berries on the bottom suffer under soft weight, becoming too bruised to eat.

When you bring them home at day's end and show them to your father — your mother still at the far edge of the forest — he looks into the buckets, takes a bite from each, and glances at your hands stained aubergine. He pauses a moment, as he savors the sunned taste on his tongue, then smiles and says: 'you've either been in another bar fight, or you've been crucified again.'

You look up, your hands blackened with another summer of berry and blood and say 'yes' to both.

>full moon
>my face without
>wisdom teeth

Hands

Her small hands, worn from work and weathered with age, were wise in the ways of making and mending. When I saw them last night, by hearth's faint light, they were folded like wings on her lap, ready, it seemed, to fly into that vast space that she kept to herself.

> compass needle
> the crow's beak
> pointing north

Hawk

During a recent mountain hike, I spotted a hawk on the trail's edge. It lay on its back, its wings open like a book half read. The fire had faded from its eyes, and its talons, curved like scythes, clutched nothing. I had no shovel, so I gathered stones and stacked them over the body, making a rough mausoleum. I wanted the vultures, which would gather, to orbit over something else dead or dying; I did want them to have this hawk, this fierce and fallen light, whose wings I had folded like a present carefully wrapped. Before I laid the last stones, I turned its head to the side like a sleeping child, so that it might better hear the earth offer its soft whispers of welcome.

> owl moon
> birds of prey soaring
> beneath my skin

Afterlife

It will be October there, a paper bag tumbling down a nameless street past a diner where a man sits, accompanied only by a newspaper in a language he cannot read. Released from a nearby asylum, long-haired men in white shirts shake feral cats from their hair. Children on stoops build kites out of the bones of their ancestors. In the distance, a parade of trombones heads towards the cemetery, where each headstone is a thumb. We all put on masks and turn towards the hoard of long-faced spirits rushing towards us; we flinch a little, as each of them calls us by name.

> closed casket
> all alone
> in the confessional

On the Road

The blackberries were blighted, but we managed to make jam anyway. Even though our teeth have been vandalized by age, and our socks have long lost their twins, we walk into a world stubborn as a mirror, where the low sky scrapes our backs.

We hold the road like a clarinet, our blackened tongues searching for the reed, the only music the treefall behind us. Our faces etched and angled like keys, we are looking for some mystery to unlock, knowing that when we do, one of us will vanish, and one of us will stay.

    braces on her teeth time to trap ghosts

Bear

Once stricken, bear resuscitated me. Now I breathe as bear breathes. The words I utter, irrepressible as bear claws. I stand on my hind legs to sniff out bears hidden in the air. My heavy scent is the world's scent, blood and honey. On the mountain nothing moves but my bear mind. I once stopped a man with a look; he fumbled before dropping. There is no line between bear and not-bear.

lark distance the subtraction of my weight

On the Line

The white shirts pinned to the clothesline are the ghosts of decapitated businessmen. Socks are quarter notes in B-flat minor dangling from the bottom of the scale. Pants are rabbit ears, stiff and upside down, listening intently for the coyote's soft footfalls. Sheets, weary of a world gone flat, flap in the breeze, delighting, for a moment, in being birds' blank wings. Pinned underwear makes a mixed family, each a mask in a story not told, but hinted at. The monochromatic towels are featureless, cleansed, waiting to soak up another week of gossip. After the laundry is taken down, birds land on the line to sun themselves and to sing of news we will never know.

> wind gust
> the sudden uplift
> of my voice

The Gator

Once when I was asleep, an alligator came into the room and stopped at the foot of the bed. Standing there, like a weight-lifter at the top of a pushup, it waited for me to awaken, to take notice, to take a position. I nudge my wife awake and tell her that there's an alligator in the house. I think to leap onto its back, which was rough as though it had been hacked with an axe, while my wife would wrap its mouth with black electrical tape. But before either of us moves, the alligator walks away, silently, its claws not even clicking on the wood floor. We rise from bed and search the house, checking our daughter's room first, and then rooms where my sisters are staying. But we do not find the alligator, after having searched the rest of the house. My wife and I double-check the windows and the doors and return to bed, but as I lie down, I feel my heart sloshing in my chest like a swamp that has been disturbed.

> foot of the bed
> our shoes still warm
> from walking

Kafka Calling

Kafka called, said, 'visit Borges.' 'But you're both dead,' I said. 'So what?' he said, 'go.'

Hitched a ride on a flight of crows angling south, landed in a maze of streets, everyone in masks, their eyes rolling like thunder, hailed a cab, felt like I was crawling inside an egg, passed by some buildings beginning to panic, came to a lurching stop, luckily I had a bag of raspberries, knocked on the door — smooth as the back of a violin — was greeted by Borges, or someone becoming Borges, who brought me into the library where, above a sleeping panther, books were singing on the shelves.

    old insurance claims the vowels of fish

Toe Stories

"Scratch your flesh raw between your toes, but you won't find the answer."
— Franz Kafka, *The Complete Stories*

Big toe of my right foot, that over-eater, blind rat craving cotton, it gnaws the skins of socks. It is a horse trying to spit the bit, straining against reins to gallop from the herd. It can gesture like an umpire or push through dirt like a mole. It is no friend of the rock. On Halloween, it dresses like a whale, going from door to door, calling out biblical names.

The second toe, the tall one, brags that it once roamed as an elephant. At night, it says, it lumbered on grassy plains, holding the moon in its trunk. It loves music, always leaping a little when a trumpet sounds.

The third is an oar yoked to other oars. Unable to row its own way, it strives to keep pace, to stay in sync, to keep the peace, to go along, not to rock the boat. It wishes it had been born a swordfish or a locomotive.

The fourth is the forgotten child, the bat that won't leave the cave, the seeing-eye-dog that went blind, the caterpillar that will not unfold into a butterfly. It may once have been a tiger's tooth but is now a clerk in an antique shop. Its home is filled with posters of mystery movies. It smokes cigarettes, when the other toes are asleep.

The fifth is the period ending the sentence. It wears a bruise from banging into furniture. It winces, but never shouts, though it longs for the hyperbole of an operatic voice. It will one day become a candle burning, while the rest of the toes melt away.

body emergency torn between reincarnations

Hinge

Slip into a hinge, that would be my move. Let someone else shrink into a key or pound and pummel with a hammer's blunt head. I am happily a hinge. From casual glance, hinge seems an open book, but no one knows how to read it: flat Braille to the blind or a blank brass slate to the eye craving words. Yet within, the hinge brims with many beings, even though the drunk slams it, or the cautious child pushes it with feather's touch; the hinge, like a butterfly's wings, opens and closes between two presses of wood or metal and sings things that most ears, like dead oak or deaf dogs, never hear.

I have heard voices seep out when hinges open and close. Perhaps there is more than mere metal inside a hinge; perhaps in hinges are sounds of lives unseen (only heard by those whose hearing folds inward): the moan of an old man rusty with morning; the hiss of a shadowy voice caught between worlds; the squeaks of bats fallen in a flat moonless sky; and the rustle of waters parting, making it safe for more in-hinged beings to quickly cross over from their world to ours.

> abandoned farm house
> the sudden need
> to open old doors

Boketto

Early morning, jasmine slapping the house, coffee next to me as I gaze through the window without purpose, as instructed. Lessons paid for but never quite learned. A mourning dove lands on the barn roof. Then another. The cream-colored cat calls at the back door. In the pond, a lone duck, leaves a v in its wake. At the edge of the field, which I might brush-hog later today, the forest of oak and elm stands like hair suddenly pushed back or like dancers hesitant to step onto the floor. The window suddenly shivers with wind.

> full moon
> the mark of a moist glass
> on the table

INVITATION

If you stand at the edge of the desert and open your arms, every particle of sand will invite you to let go of the parts of you that you no longer need. Notice that rocks do not mourn their slow shift into sediment, nor do the arroyos curse the sky after their waters turn to dust, and the cactus wren does not grumble about its charred song. Stop and let yourself be like the rockcolored lizard, still as stone, and allow the long days of wind and breath to gradually wear you away.

> river blossom
> the blue heron
> on one leg

Acknowledgments

Some of these haibun have appeared in *The Haibun Journal, Contemporary Haibun Online, Haibun Today, Drifting Sands Haibun, Presence, Frogpond, The Akitsu Quarterly, Chrysanthemum, Prune Juice, Sonic Boom,* and *Human/Kind.*

KEITH POLETTE lives and writes in El Paso, Texas.